GETTING TO KNOW
THE U.S. PRESIDENTS

FRANKLIN D. ROOSEVELT

THIRTY-SECOND PRESIDENT
1933 – 1945

WRITTEN AND ILLUSTRATED BY MIKE VENEZIA

CHILDREN'S PRESS
AN IMPRINT OF SCHOLASTIC INC.
NEW YORK   TORONTO   LONDON   AUCKLAND   SYDNEY
MEXICO CITY   NEW DELHI   HONG KONG
DANBURY, CONNECTICUT

Reading Consultant: Nanci R. Vargus, Ed.D., Assistant Professor, School of Education, University of Indianapolis

Historical Consultant: Marc J. Selverstone, Ph.D., Assistant Professor, Miller Center of Public Affairs, University of Virginia

Photographs © 2007: AP/Wide World Photos: 3; Art Resource, NY/Smithsonian American Art Museum, Washington, DC: 27; Corbis Images: 13, 22, 23, 24, 29, 32 (Bettmann), 30, 31; Danita Delimont Stock Photography/Julie Eggers: 20; Franklin D. Roosevelt Library: 8 top, 8 bottom, 9, 14, 15, 16, 21, 26; Getty Images/MPI: 19; The Oakland Museum of California, City of Oakand, ₱ the Dorothea Lange Collection, Gift of Paul S. Taylor: 5.

Colorist for illustrations: Andrew Day

Library of Congress Cataloging-in-Publication Data

Venezia, Mike.
   Franklin D. Roosevelt / written and illustrated by Mike Venezia.
      p. cm. — (Getting to know the U.S. Presidents)
   ISBN-13: 978-0-516-22636-1 (lib. bdg.)   978-0-531-17945-1 (pbk.)
   ISBN-10: 0-516-22636-3 (lib. bdg.)   0-531-17945-1 (pbk.)
   1. Roosevelt, Franklin D. (Franklin Delano), 1882-1945—Juvenile literature. 2. Presidents—United States—Biography—Juvenile literature. I. Title. II. Series.

   E807.V46 2007
   973.917092—dc22
   [B]

2006023352

1 2 3 4 5 6 7 8 9 10 R 17 16 15 14 13 12 11 10 09 08

President Franklin D. Roosevelt at the wheel of his car

Franklin Delano Roosevelt was the thirty-second president of the United States. He was born on January 30, 1882, at his family's home in Hyde Park, New York. Many people think Franklin Roosevelt was one of the greatest presidents ever. Franklin guided the United States through two of its biggest challenges, the Great Depression and World War II.

The Great Depression began in 1929 and lasted almost twelve years. It was a period when millions of people lost their jobs, homes, savings, and, worst of all, hope.

There were many reasons for the Great Depression. For instance, lots of people borrowed money from banks, and lost it all by making foolish investments. Farmers had grown way too many crops, and could hardly make any money selling their grain, corn, and other products. Soon they lost their farms.

Not everyone was poor, though. Some owners of big businesses paid their workers very little and kept huge profits for themselves.

White Angel Bread Line, a photograph by Dorothea Lange showing people waiting in a soup line during the Great Depression

This only made it harder for average working people to buy products and pay back their debts. Soon banks, stores, and factories went out of business too.

It took a terrible event like World War II to finally end the Great Depression. The United States entered World War II after Japan attacked Pearl Harbor, Hawaii, on December 7, 1941. Right away, millions of American workers were needed to help build fighter planes, tanks, warships, trucks, and weapons of all kinds.

Suddenly, factories were operating twenty-four hours a day. Many other Americans went to work in a different way. They were drafted into or joined the army and navy. Americans fought in Europe, Africa, Asia, and in the Pacific. The Great Depression eased up as World War II began. Only an outstanding president like Franklin Roosevelt could have kept the nation together during these difficult times.

Young Franklin sitting on a donkey with his pet dog, Budgy

Franklin Delano Roosevelt had a remarkable childhood. The Roosevelts were rich. Mr. and Mrs. Roosevelt loved their only child and were very protective of him. Franklin was schooled at home on his family's large estate in Hyde Park, New York. The Roosevelts also had a big summer house by the sea.

Franklin at age ten

Eleven-year-old Franklin
with his mother, Sara

Franklin always had everything he needed while he was growing up, including a donkey, pet dogs, and a pony. Mr. Roosevelt taught his son to ride, hunt, and sail. Franklin loved to collect stamps, stuff and mount birds, and build model ships, especially navy ships. Even though Franklin's parents spoiled him, they taught him to always respect and help others who were less fortunate. Franklin was a very charming and polite boy.

When Franklin was fourteen years old, he was sent to the Groton School, a ritzy boy's school in Massachusetts. It was the first time he was away from his parents. Even though it took a while, Franklin finally adjusted to his new school. He was only a so-so student there, however.

He was also just an average student when he went to college at Harvard. He did much better outside of class, joining lots of clubs and becoming the editor of Harvard's newspaper, *The Crimson*.

While Franklin was at Harvard, his father died. It was a very sad time for him. Mr. Roosevelt had been more than a father. He had been a companion and teacher as well. Franklin began looking to his older cousin, Teddy Roosevelt, as a role model. Teddy had been governor of New York and soon would become president of the United States. Franklin admired Teddy's exciting new ideas about how to run the government. He began to think about a life in politics, too.

Theodore Roosevelt, shown here giving a campaign
speech, was a role model for his cousin Franklin.

Eleanor Roosevelt in her wedding dress

Franklin had another cousin he became very interested in. Eleanor Roosevelt was a distant cousin Franklin had met at family gatherings over the years. Franklin and Eleanor always got along well.

Eleanor Roosevelt spent her life working hard for the rights of children, women, and minorities. Here she hands out Christmas presents at a school she helped support for underprivileged boys in New York City.

Now that they were grown up, they found they were crazy about each other. Eventually, Franklin and Eleanor decided to get married. Eleanor would someday become an excellent First Lady. She used her position to help needy Americans, and became very famous on her own.

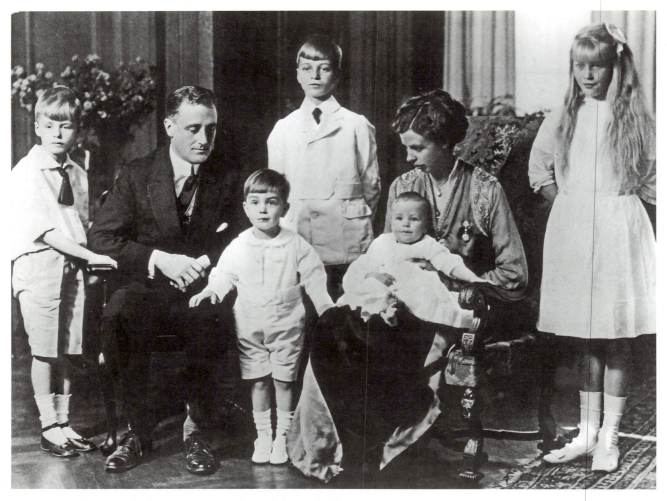

Franklin and Eleanor Roosevelt and their children in 1916

Franklin and Eleanor had six children, one of whom died as an infant. As busy as she was raising a family, Eleanor spent much of her time helping Franklin win elections. Before getting into politics, Franklin tried being a lawyer for a while. He found that law bored him stiff, though.

In 1910, when members of New York's Democratic Party asked him to run for state senator, Franklin was thrilled. Instead of campaigning around his district by horse and buggy, he rented a bright red convertible. Because cars were a new invention at the time, Franklin attracted a lot of attention. People liked the friendly, hardworking Franklin, and he won the election.

As a New York state senator, Franklin was able to help support his favorite nominee for president, Woodrow Wilson. When Wilson became president, he rewarded Franklin by offering him a job as assistant secretary of the navy. Franklin had always loved anything having to do with the navy.

Franklin studied U.S. naval history in school, and had enjoyed building model navy ships. When the country entered World War I, Franklin successfully helped guide the U.S. Navy through the war. Soon after the war ended in 1918, Franklin left his navy job to run for vice president with the Democratic presidential nominee, James M. Cox.

A 1920 campaign poster for James M. Cox for president and Franklin Delano Roosevelt for vice president

Cox and Roosevelt lost the election of 1920, and Franklin went back to being a lawyer. During a very busy period, Franklin felt he needed a rest. He left New York City and went to his family's summer home on Campobello Island. It was there that Franklin was struck with polio.

The Roosevelt summer home at Campobello Island in New Brunswick, Canada

Franklin and Eleanor relaxing on the beach at Campobello before Franklin was struck with polio

Before a vaccine was invented, polio was a horrible disease that disabled thousands of people every year. Most of them were children.

Franklin suddenly found himself unable to walk. He could have just given up and had other people take care of him for the rest of his life. But Franklin Roosevelt made up his mind to fight his disease.

Franklin Roosevelt (center) exercises in the water with other patients at the polio treatment center he founded in Warm Springs, Georgia.

With the help of his family and friends, Franklin exercised and learned to get around without the use of his legs. Franklin decided not only to try to lead a normal life, but to get back into politics.

Franklin had always cared about the well being of poor Americans. Now he knew how people *really* felt when they were suffering

Although Roosevelt did learn to move his legs and was often photographed standing up, his legs remained paralyzed for the rest of his life.

and needed help. Franklin Roosevelt went on to be elected governor of New York State. He showed great spirit, energy, and good humor. People liked him so much, they hardly noticed or cared that Franklin had a hard time moving around.

Franklin Roosevelt was governor of New York when the Great Depression began. Right away, he began to think of creative ways to help hungry, unemployed people of his state. By the time 1932 rolled around, Franklin was getting a lot of national attention. Democratic Party leaders decided to ask Franklin to run for president. Franklin couldn't wait to start campaigning.

President Herbert Hoover (left) and President-elect Franklin Roosevelt (right) on the way to Roosevelt's inauguration on March 4, 1933

Franklin, who was often known by his initials, FDR, ran against President Herbert Hoover. To many people, Herbert Hoover seemed like a worn-out leader who had given up trying to solve the problems of the Depression. The confident, energetic FDR promised to fix things and seemed like a burst of sunshine. FDR easily won the election.

President Roosevelt started out like a shot out of a cannon! He and his cabinet members helped get Congress to pass dozens of new laws to fight the Depression. Some of these laws set up programs that put Americans back to work building roads, bridges, dams, schools, and public parks while being paid by the government.

The Civilian Conservation Corps was a New Deal program that took unemployed young men off city streets and put them to work in forests and national parks. Here, CCC workers clear land to plant trees in Oregon.

The WPA was a New Deal program that gave jobs to some two million workers, including artists. They created huge murals for public spaces, such as the one above, painted for the post office in Anson, Texas.

Some programs put thousands of artists and writers to work, too. Other laws helped fix the nation's banks. All of these laws together were known as the New Deal. They did a lot to move the country out of the Great Depression. What helped more than anything, though, was FDR's self-confidence and belief in the future.

President Roosevelt often spoke to the American people over the radio. These friendly talks became known as "fireside chats." They filled everyone in on what the president was doing and how things were going in the country. People felt that President Roosevelt was almost like a guest sitting with them in their homes.

Fireside chats really came in handy during World War II. When Japan attacked the United States at Pearl Harbor, it was a very scary time. President Roosevelt's fireside chats did a lot to reassure people and give them hope.

FDR giving one of his "fireside chats"

During World War II, the United States joined forces with Great Britain and the Soviet Union to fight Nazi Germany and Fascist Italy in Europe and Africa, and to fight Japan in the Pacific. FDR chose excellent generals to head up the army and navy. Even so, things went poorly at first. Eventually, though, after three years of fighting, it looked like Germany and Japan would lose the war.

U.S. Army troops move into Bonn, Germany, during the fall of Germany at the end of World War II in 1945.

American fighter pilots running to their planes in the Pacific during World War II

President Roosevelt began to make plans about what to do when the war ended. He wanted to make sure bombed-out cities and countries would be rebuilt properly. He also wanted to find a way to keep lasting world peace. FDR didn't live to see the end of the war, though. On April 12, 1945, just a few weeks before Germany surrendered, Franklin Roosevelt collapsed and died of a stroke.

FDR giving the victory sign

FDR was elected to four four-year terms. That's more terms than any other president in U.S. history. The American people felt they needed FDR's leadership during a Great Depression and a world war.

FDR wasn't a perfect president. Some critics even accused him of abusing his power and influence. For example, after Japan bombed Pearl Harbor, many people feared and mistrusted Japanese Americans. FDR made a bad decision by sending thousands of innocent Japanese American citizens to prisonlike camps until the war ended. Still, most people were quite happy to have had a strong, remarkable leader when one was needed.